Book 1
Android Programming In a Day!
BY SAM KEY

&

Book 2
MYSQL Programming
Professional Made Easy
BY SAM KEY

Book 1
Android Programming In a Day!

BY SAM KEY

The Power Guide for Beginners In Android App Programming

**Programming Box Set #78: Android Programming in a Day & MySQL
Programming Professional Made Easy**

Table Of Contents

Introduction

I want to thank you and congratulate you for purchasing the book, "Introduction to Android Programming in a Day – The Power Guide for Beginners in Android App Programming".

This book contains proven steps and strategies on how to get started with Android app development.

This book will focus on preparing you with the fun and tiring world of Android app development. Take note that this book will not teach you on how to program. It will revolve around the familiarization of the Android SDK and Eclipse IDE.

Why not focus on programming immediately? Unfortunately, the biggest reason many aspiring Android developers stop on learning this craft is due to the lack of wisdom on the Android SDK and Eclipse IDE.

Sure, you can also make apps using other languages like Python and other IDEs on the market. However, you can expect that it is much more difficult than learning Android's SDK and Eclipse's IDE.

On the other hand, you can use tools online to develop your Android app for you. But where's the fun in that? You will not learn if you use such tools. Although it does not mean that you should completely stay away from that option.

Anyway, the book will be split into four chapters. The first will prepare you and tell you the things you need before you develop apps. The second will tell you how you can configure your project. The third will introduce you to the Eclipse IDE. And the last chapter will teach you on how to run your program in your Android device.

Also, this book will be sprinkled with tidbits about the basic concepts of Android app development. And as you read along, you will have an idea on what to do next.

Thanks again for purchasing this book, I hope you enjoy it!

Chapter 1: Preparation

Android application development is not easy. You must have some decent background in program development. It is a plus if you know Visual Basic and Java. And it will be definitely a great advantage if you are familiar or have already used Eclipse's IDE (Integrated Development Environment). Also, being familiar with XML will help you.

You will need a couple of things before you can start developing apps.

First, you will need a high-end computer. It is common that other programming development kits do not need a powerful computer in order to create applications. However, creating programs for Android is a bit different. You will need more computing power for you to run Android emulators, which are programs that can allow you to test your programs in your computer.

Using a weak computer without a decent processor and a good amount of RAM will only make it difficult for you to run those emulators. If you were able to run it, it will run slowly.

Second, you will need an Android device. That device will be your beta tester. With it, you will know how your program will behave in an Android device. When choosing the test device, make sure that it is at par with the devices of the market you are targeting for your app. If you are targeting tablet users, use a tablet. If you are targeting smartphones, then use a smartphone.

Third, you will need the Android SDK (Software Development Kit) from Google. The SDK is a set of files and programs that can allow you to create and compile your program's code. As of this writing, the latest Android SDK's file size is around 350mb. It will take you 15 – 30 minutes to download it. If you uncompressed the Android SDK file, it will take up around 450mb of your computer's disk space. The link to the download page is: http://developer.android.com/sdk/index.html

The SDK can run on Windows XP, Windows 7, Mac OSX 10.8.5 (or higher), and Linux distros that can run 32bit applications and has glibc (GNU C library) 2.11 or higher.

Once you have unpacked the contents of the file you downloaded, open the SDK Manager. That program is the development kit's update tool. To make sure you have the latest versions of the kit's components, run the manager once in a while and download those updates. Also, you can use the SDK Manager to download older versions of SDK. You must do that in case you want to make programs with devices with dated Android operating systems.

Chapter 2: Starting Your First Project

To start creating programs, you will need to open Eclipse. The Eclipse application file can be found under the eclipse folder on the extracted files from the Android SDK. Whenever you run Eclipse, it will ask you where you want your Eclipse workspace will be stored. You can just use the default location and just toggle the don't show checkbox.

New Project

To start a new Android application project, just click on the dropdown button of the New button on Eclipse's toolbar. A context menu will appear, and click on the Android application project.

The New Android Application project details window will appear. In there, you will need to input some information for your project. You must provide your program's application name, project name, and package name. Also, you can configure the minimum and target SDK where your program can run and the SDK that will be used to compile your code. And lastly, you can indicate the default theme that your program will use.

Application Name

The application name will be the name that will be displayed on the Google's Play Store when you post it there. The project name will be more of a file name for Eclipse. It will be the project's identifier. It should be unique for every project that you build in Eclipse. By default, Eclipse will generate a project and package name for your project when you type something in the Application Name text box.

Package Name

The package name is not usually displayed for users. Take note that in case you will develop a large program, you must remember that your package name should never be changed. On the other hand, it is common that package names are the reverse of your domain name plus your project's name. For example, if your website's domain name is www.mywebsite.com and your project's name is Hello World, a good package name for your project will be com.mywebsite.helloworld.

The package name should follow the Java package name convention. The naming convention is there to prevent users from having similar names, which could result to numerous conflicts. Some of the rules you need to follow for the package name are:

•   Your package name should be all in lower caps. Though Eclipse will accept a package name with a capital letter, but it is still best to adhere to standard practice.

•   The reverse domain naming convention is included as a standard practice.

•   Avoid using special characters in the package name. Instead, you can replace it with underscores.

•   Also, you should never use or include the default com.example in your package name. Google Play will not accept an app with a package name like that.

Minimum SDK

Minimum required SDK could be set to lower or the lowest version of Android. Anything between the latest and the set minimum required version can run your program. Setting it to the lowest, which is API 1 or Android 1.0, can make your target audience wider.

Setting it to Android 2.2 (Froyo) or API 8, can make your program run on almost 95% of all Android devices in the world. The drawback fn this is that the features you can include in your program will be limited. Adding new features will force your minimum required SDK to move higher since some of the new functions in Android is not available on lower versions of the API (Application Programming Interface).

Target SDK

The target SDK should be set to the version of Android that most of your target audience uses. It indicates that you have tested your program to that version. And it means that your program is fully functional if they use it on a device that runs the target Android version.

Whenever a new version of Android appears, you should also update the target SDK of your program. Of course, before you release it to the market again, make sure that you test it on an updated device.

If a device with the same version as your set target SDK runs your program, it will not do any compatibility behavior or adjust itself to run the program. By default, you should set it to the highest version to attract your potential app buyers. Setting a lower version for your target SDK would make your program old and dated. By the way, the target SDK should be always higher or equal with the minimum target SDK version.

Compile with

The compile with version should be set to the latest version of Android. This is to make sure that your program will run on almost all versions down to the minimum version you have indicated, and to take advantage of the newest features and optimization offered by the latest version of Android. By default, the Android SDK will only have one version available for this option, which is API 20 or Android 4.4 (KitKat Wear).

After setting those all up, it is time to click on the Next button. The new page in the screen will contain some options such as creating custom launcher icon and creating activity. As of now, you do not need to worry about those. Just leave the default values and check, and click the Next button once again.

Custom Launcher Icon

Since you have left the Create Custom Launcher option checked, the next page will bring you in the launcher icon customization page. In there, you will be given three options on how you would create your launcher. Those options are launcher icons made from an image, clipart, or text.

With the text and clipart method, you can easily create an icon you want without thinking about the size and quality of the launcher icon. With those two, you can just get a preset image from the SDK or Android to use as a launcher icon. The same goes with the text method since all you need is to type the letters you want to appear on the icon and the SDK will generate an icon based on that.

The launcher icon editor also allows you to change the background and foreground color of your icon. Also, you can scale the text and clipart by changing the value of the additional padding of the icon. And finally, you can add simple 3D shapes on your icon to make it appear more professional.

Bitmap Iconography Tips

When it comes to images, you need to take note of a few reminders. First, always make sure that you will use vector images. Unlike the typical bitmap images (pictures taken from cameras or images created using Paint), vector images provide accurate and sharp images. You can scale it multiple times, but its sharpness will not disappear and will not pixelate. After all, vector images do not contain information about pixels. It only has numbers and location of the colors and lines that will appear in it. When it is scaled, it does not perform antialiasing or stretching since its image will be mathematically rendered.

In case that you will be the one creating or designing the image that you will use for your program and you will be creating a bitmap image, make sure that you start with a large image. A large image is easier to create and design.

Also, since in Android, multiple sizes of your icon will be needed, a large icon can make it easier for you to make smaller ones. Take note that if you scale a big picture into a small one, some details will be lost, but it will be easier to edit and fix and it will still look crisp. On the other hand, if you scale a small image into a big one, it will pixelate and insert details that you do not intend to show such as jagged and blurred edges.

Nevertheless, even when scaling down a big image into a smaller one, do not forget to rework the image. Remember that a poor-looking icon makes people think that the app you are selling is low-quality. And again, if you do not want to go through all that, create a vector image instead.

Also, when you create an image, make sure that it will be visible in any background. Aside from that, it is advisable to make it appear uniform with other Android icons. To do that, make sure that your image has a distinct silhouette that will make it look like a 3D image. The icon should appear as if you were looking above it and as if the source of light is on top of the image. The topmost part of the icon should appear lighter and the bottom part should appear darker.

Activity

Once you are done with your icon, click on the Next button. The page will now show the Activity window. It will provide you with activity templates to work on. The window has a preview box where you can see what your app will look like for every activity template. Below the selection, there is a description box that will tell you what each template does. For now, select the Blank Activity and click Next. The next page will ask you some details regarding the activity. Leave it on its default values and click Finish.

Once you do that, Eclipse will setup your new project. It might take a lot of time, especially if you are using a dated computer. The next chapter will discuss the programming interface of Eclipse.

Chapter 3: Getting Familiar with Eclipse and Contents of an Android App

When Eclipse has finished its preparation, you will be able to start doing something to your program. But hold onto your horses; explore Eclipse first before you start fiddling with anything.

Editing Area

In the middle of the screen, you will see a preview of your program. In it, you will see your program's icon beside the title of your program. Just left of it is the palette window. It contains all the elements that you can place in your program.

Both of these windows are inside Eclipse's editing area. You will be spending most of your time here, especially if you are going to edit or view something in your code or layout.

The form widgets tab will be expanded in the palette by default. There you will see the regular things you see in an Android app such as buttons, radio buttons, progress bar (the circle icon that spins when something is loading in your device or the bar the fills up when your device is loading), seek bar, and the ratings bar (the stars you see in reviews).

Aside from the form widgets, there are other elements that you can check and use. Press the horizontal tabs or buttons and examine all the elements you can possibly use in your program.

To insert a widget in your program, you can just drag the element you want to include from the palette and drop it in your program's preview. Eclipse will provide you visual markers and grid snaps for you to place the widgets you want on the exact place you want. Easy, right?

Take note, some of the widgets on the palette may require higher-level APIs or versions of Android. For example, the Grid Layout from the Layouts section of the palette requires API 14 (Android 4.0 Ice Cream Sandwich) or higher. If you add it in your program, it will ask you if you want to install it. In case you did include and install it, remember that it will not be compatible for older versions or any device running on API 13 and lower. It is advisable that you do not include any element that asks for installation. It might result into errors.

Output Area, Status Bar, and Problem Browser

On the bottom part of Eclipse, the status bar, problem browser, and output area can be found. It will contain messages regarding to the state of your project. If Eclipse found errors in your program, it will be listed there. Always check the Problems bar for any issues. Take note that you cannot run or compile your program if Eclipse finds at least one error on your project.

Navigation Pane

On the leftmost part of your screen is the navigation pane that contains the package explorer. The package explorer lets you browse all the files that are included in your project. Three of the most important files that you should know where to look for are:

•   activity_main.xml: This file is your program's main page or window. And it will be the initial file that will be opened when you create a new project. In case you accidentally close it on your editor window, you can find it at: YourProjectName > res > layout > activity_main.xml.

• MainActivity.java: As of now, you will not need to touch this file. However, it is important to know where it is since later in your Android development activities, you will need to understand it and its contents. It is located at: YourProjectName > src > YourPackageName > MainActivity.java.

• AndroidManifest.xml: It contains the essential information that you have set up a while ago when you were creating your project file in Eclipse. You can edit the minimum and target SDK in there. It is located at YourProjectName > AndroidManifest.xml.

Aside from those files, you should take note of the following directories:

• src/: This is where most of your program's source files will be placed. And your main activity file is locafile is located.

• res/: Most of the resources will be placed here. The resources are placed inside the subdirectories under this folder.

• res/drawable-hdpi/: Your high density bitmap files that you might show in your app will go in here.

• res/layout/: All the pages or interface in your app will be located here – including your activity_main.xml.

• res/values/: The values you will store and use in your program will be placed in this directory in form of XML files.

In the event that you will create multiple projects, remember that the directory for those other projects aside from the one you have opened will still be available in your package explorer. Because of that, you might get confused over the files you are working on. Thankfully, Eclipse's title bar indicates the location and name of the file you are editing, which makes it easier to know what is currently active on the editing area.

Outline Box

Displays the current structure of the file you are editing. The outline panel will help you visualize the flow and design of your app. Also, it can help you find the widgets you want to edit.

Properties Box

Whenever you are editing a layout file, the properties box will appear below the outline box. With the properties box, you can edit certain characteristics of a widget. For example, if you click on the Hello World text on the preview of your main activity layout file, the contents of the properties box will be populated. In there, you can edit the properties of the text element that you have clicked. You can change the text, height, width, and even its font color.

Menu and Toolbar

The menu bar contains all the major functionalities of Eclipse. In case you do not know where the button of a certain tool is located, you can just invoke that tool's function on the menu bar. On the other hand, the tool bar houses all the major functions in Eclipse. The most notable buttons there are the New, Save, and Run.

As of now, look around Eclipse's interface. Also, do not do or change anything on the main activity file or any other file. The next chapter will discuss about how to run your program. As of now, the initial contents of your project are also valid as an android program. Do not change anything since you might produce an unexpected error. Nevertheless, if you really do want to change something, go ahead. You can just create another project for you to keep up with the next chapter.

Chapter 4: Running Your Program

By this time, even if you have not done anything yet to your program, you can already run and test it in your Android device or emulator. Why teach this first before the actual programming? Well, unlike typical computer program development, Android app development is a bit bothersome when it comes to testing.

First, the program that you are developing is intended for Android devices. You cannot actually run it normally in your computer without the help of an emulator. And you will actually do a lot of testing. Even with the first lines of code or changes in your program, you will surely want to test it.

Second, the Android emulator works slow. Even with good computers, the emulator that comes with the Android SDK is painstakingly sluggish. Alternatively, you can use BlueStacks. BlueStacks is a free Android emulator that works better than the SDK's emulator. It can even run games with it! However, it is buggy and does not work well (and does not even run sometimes) with every computer.

This chapter will focus on running your program into your Android device. You will need to have a USB data cable and connect your computer and Android. Also, you will need to have the right drivers for your device to work as a testing platform for the programs you will develop. Unfortunately, this is the preferred method for most beginners since running your app on Android emulators can bring a lot more trouble since it is super slow. And that might even discourage you to continue Android app development.

Why Android Emulators are Slow

Why are Android emulators slow? Computers can run virtual OSs without any problems, but why cannot the Android emulator work fine? Running virtual OSs is not something as resource-extensive anymore with today's computer standards. However, with Android, you will actually emulate an OS together with a mobile device. And nowadays, these mobile devices are as powerful as some of the dated computers back then. Regular computers will definitely have a hard time with that kind of payload from an Android emulator.

USB Debugging Mode

To run your program in an Android device, connect your Android to your computer. After that, set your Android into USB debugging mode. Depending on the version of the Android device you are using, the steps might change.

For 3.2 and older Android devices:

Go to Settings > Applications > Development

For 4.0 and newer Android devices:

Go to Settings > Developer Options

For 4.2 and newer Android devices with hidden Developer Options:

Go to Settings > About Phone. After that, tap the Build Number seven times. Go back to the previous screen. The Developer Options should be visible now.

Android Device Drivers

When USB debugging is enabled, your computer will install the right drivers for the Android device that you have. If your computer does not have the right drivers, you will not be able to run your program on your device. If that happens to you, visit this page: http://developer.android.com/tools/extras/oem-usb.html.   It contains instructions on how you can install the right driver for your device and operating system.

Running an App in Your Android Device Using Eclipse

Once your device is already connected and you have the right drivers for it, you can now do a test run of your application. On your Eclipse window, click the Run button on the toolbar or in the menu bar.

If a Run As window appeared, select the Android Application option and click on the OK button. After that, a dialog box will appear. It will provide you with two options: running the program on an Android device or on an AVD (Android Virtual Device) or emulator.

If your device was properly identified by your computer, it will appear on the list. Click on your device's name and click OK. Eclipse will compile your Android app, install it on your device, and then run it. That is how simple it is.

Take note, there will be times that your device will appear offline on the list. In case that happens, there are two simple fixes that you can do to make it appear online again: restart your device or disable and enable the USB debugging function on your device.

Now, you can start placing widgets on your main activity file. However, always make sure that you do not place any widgets that require higher APIs.

Conclusion

Thank you again for purchasing this book!

I hope this book was able to help you get started with Android Programming in a Day!.

The next step is to study the following:

View and Viewgroups: View and Viewgroups are the two types of objects that you will be dealing with Android. View objects are the elements or widgets that you see in Android programs. Viewgroup objects act as containers to those View objects.

Relative, Linear, and Table Layout: When it comes to designing your app, you need to know the different types of layouts. In later versions of Android, you can use other versions of layouts, but of course, the API requirements will go up if you use them. Master these, and you will be able to design faster and cleaner.

Adding Activities or Interface: Of course, you would not want your program to contain one page only. You need more. You must let your app customers to see more content and functions. In order to do that, you will need to learn adding activities to your program. This is the part when developing your Android app will be tricky. You will not be able to rely completely on the drag and drop function and graphical layout view of Eclipse. You will need to start typing some code into your program.

Adding the Action Bar: The action bar is one of the most useful elements in Android apps. It provides the best location for the most used functions in your program. And it also aid your users when switching views, tabs, or drop down list.

Once you have gain knowledge on those things, you will be able to launch a decent app on the market. The last thing you might want to do is to learn how to make your program support other Android devices.

You must know very well that Android devices come in all shapes and form. An Android device can be a tablet, a smartphone, or even a television. Also, they come with different screen sizes. You cannot just expect that all your customers will be using a 4-inch display smartphone. Also, you should think about the versions of Android they are using. Lastly, you must also add language options to your programs. Even though English is fine, some users will appreciate if your program caters to the primary language that they use.

And that is about it for this book. Make sure you do not stop learning Android app development.

Finally, if you enjoyed this book, please take the time to share your thoughts and post a review on Amazon. We do our best to reach out to readers and provide the best value we can. Your positive review will help us achieve that. It'd be greatly appreciated!

Thank you and good luck!

Book 2
MYSQL Programming
Professional Made Easy

BY SAM KEY

Expert MYSQL Programming Language Success in a Day for any Computer User!

Table Of Contents

Introduction

I want to thank you and congratulate you for purchasing the book, "MYSQL Programming Professional Made Easy: Expert MYSQL Programming Language Success in a Day for any Computer User!".

This book contains proven steps and strategies on how to manage MySQL databases.

The book will teach you the fundamentals of SQL and how to apply it on MySQL. It will cover the basic operations such as creating and deleting tables and databases. Also, it will tell you how to insert, update, and delete records in MySQL. In the last part of the book, you will be taught on how to connect to your MySQL server and send queries to your database using PHP.

Thankfully, by this time, this subject is probably a piece of cake for you since you might already have experienced coding in JavaScript and PHP, which are prerequisites to learning MySQL.

However, it does not mean that you will have a difficult time learning MySQL if you do not have any idea on those two scripting languages. In this book, you will learn about SQL, which works a bit different from programming languages.

Being knowledgeable alone with SQL can give you a solid idea on how MySQL and other RDBMS work. Anyway, thanks again for purchasing this book, I hope you enjoy it!

Chapter 1: Introduction to MySQL

This book will assume that you are already knowledgeable about PHP. It will focus on database application on the web. The examples here will use PHP as the main language to use to access a MySQL database. Also, this will be focused on Windows operating system users.

As of now, MySQL is the most popular database system by PHP programmers. Also, it is the most popular database system on the web. A few of the websites that use MySQL to store their data are Facebook, Wikipedia, and Twitter.

Commonly, MySQL databases are ran on web servers. Because of that, you need to use a server side scripting language to use it.

A few of the good points of MySQL against other database systems are it is scalable (it is good to use in small or large scale applications), fast, easy to use, and reliable. Also, if you are already familiar with SQL, you will not have any problems in manipulating MySQL databases.

Preparation

In the first part of this book, you will learn SQL or Standard Query Language. If you have a database program, such as Microsoft Access, installed in your computer, you can use it to practice and apply the statements you will learn.

In case you do not, you have two options. Your first option is to get a hosting account package that includes MySQL and PHP. If you do not want to spend tens of dollars for a paid web hosting account, you can opt for a free one. However, be informed that most of them will impose limitations or add annoyances, such as ads, in your account. Also, some of them have restrictions that will result to your account being banned once you break one of them.

Your second option is to get XAMMP, a web server solution that includes Apache, MySQL, and PHP. It will turn your computer into a local web server. And with it, you can play around with your MySQL database and the PHP codes you want to experiment with. Also, it

comes with phpMyAdmin. A tool that will be discussed later in this
book.

Chapter 2: Database and SQL

What is a database? A database is an application or a file wherein you can store data. It is used and included in almost all types of computer programs. A database is usually present in the background whether the program is a game, a word processor, or a website.

A database can be a storage location for a player's progress and setting on a game. It can be a storage location for dictionaries and preferences in word processors. And it can be a storage location for user accounts and page content in websites.

There are different types and forms of databases. A spreadsheet can be considered a database. Even a list of items in a text file can be considered one, too. However, unlike the database that most people know or familiar with, those kinds of databases are ideal for small applications.

RDBMS

The type of database that is commonly used for bigger applications is RDBMS or relational database management system. MySQL is an RDBMS. Other RDBMS that you might have heard about are Oracle database, Microsoft Access, and SQL Server.

Inside an RDBMS, there are tables that are composed of rows, columns, and indexes. Those tables are like spreadsheets. Each cell in a table holds a piece of data. Below is an example table:

id	username	password	email	firstname	lastname
1	Johnnyxxx	123abc	jjxxx@gmail.com	Johnny	Stew
2	cutiepatutie	qwertyuiop	cuteme@yahoo.com	Sara	Britch

3	masterm iller	theGear 12	mgshades@g mail.com	Maste r	Mi r
4	j_sasaki	H9fmaN Ca	j_sasaki@gm ail.com	Johnn y	Sa i

Note: this same table will be used as the main reference of all the examples in this book. Also, developers usually encrypt their passwords in their databases. They are not encrypted for the sake of an example.

In the table, which the book will refer to as the account table under the sample database, there are six columns (or fields) and they are id, username, password, email, firstname, and lastname. As of now, there are only four rows. Rows can be also called entries or records. Take note that the first row is not part of the count. They are just there to represent the name of the columns as headers.

An RDBMS table can contain one or more tables.

Compared to other types of databases, RDBMS are easier to use and manage because it comes with a standardized set of method when it comes to accessing and manipulating data. And that is SQL or Standard Query Language.

SQL

Before you start learning MySQL, you must familiarize yourself with SQL or Standard Query Language first. SQL is a language used to manipulate and access relational database management systems. It is not that complicated compared to learning programming languages.

Few of the things you can do with databases using SQL are:

- Get, add, update, and delete data from databases

- Create, modify, and delete databases

- Modify access permissions in databases

Most database programs use SQL as the standard method of accessing databases, but expect that some of them have a bit of variations. Some statements have different names or keywords while some have different methods to do things. Nevertheless, most of the usual operations are the same for most of them.

A few of the RDBMS that you can access using SQL – with little alterations – are MySQL, SQL Server, and Microsoft Access.

Chapter 3: SQL Syntax

SQL is like a programming language. It has its own set of keywords and syntax rules. Using SQL is like talking to the database. With SQL, you can pass on commands to the database in order for it to present and manipulate the data it contains for you. And you can do that by passing queries and statements to it.

SQL is commonly used interactively in databases. As soon as you send a query or statement, the database will process it immediately. You can perform some programming in SQL, too. However, it is much easier to leave the programming part to other programming languages. In the case of MySQL, it is typical that most of the programming is done with PHP, which is the most preferred language to use with it.

SQL's syntax is simple. Below is an example:

SELECT username FROM account

In the example, the query is commanding the database to get all the data under the username column from the account table. The database will reply with a recordset or a collection of records.

In MySQL, databases will also return the number of rows it fetched and the duration that it took to fetch the result.

Case Sensitivity

As you can see, the SQL query is straightforward and easy to understand. Also, take note that unlike PHP, MySQL is not case sensitive. Even if you change the keyword SELECT's case to select, it will still work. For example:

seLeCT username from account

However, as a standard practice, it is best that you type keywords on uppercase and values in lowercase.

Line Termination

In case that you will perform or send consecutive queries or a multiline query, you need to place a semicolon at the end of each statement to separate them. By the way, MySQL does not consider a line to be a statement when it sees a new line character – meaning, you can place other parts of your queries on multiple lines. For example:

SELECT

username

FROM

account;

New lines are treated like a typical whitespace (spaces and tabs) character. And the only accepted line terminator is a semicolon. In some cases, semicolons are not needed to terminate a line.

Chapter 4: SQL Keywords and Statements

When you memorize the SQL keywords, you can say that you are already know SQL or MySQL. Truth be told, you will be mostly using only a few SQL keywords for typical database management. And almost half of the queries you will be making will be SELECT queries since retrieving data is always the most used operation in databases.

Before you learn that, you must know how to create a database first.

CREATE DATABASE

Creating a database is simple. Follow the syntax below:

CREATE DATABASE <name of database>;

To create the sample database where the account table is located, this is all you need to type:

CREATE DATABASE sample;

Easy, right? However, an empty database is a useless database. You cannot enter any data to it yet since you do not have tables yet.

CREATE TABLE

Creating a table requires a bit of planning. Before you create a table, you must already know the columns you want to include in it. Also, you need to know the size, type, and other attributes of the pieces of data that you will insert on your columns. Once you do, follow the syntax below:

CREATE TABLE <name of table>

(

<name of column 1> <data type(size)> <attributes>,

<name of column 2> <data type(size)> <attributes>,

<name of column 3> <data type(size)> <attributes>

);

By the way, you cannot just create a table out of nowhere. To make sure that the table you will create will be inside a database, you must be connected to one. Connection to databases will be discussed in the later part of this book. As of now, imagine that you are now connected to the sample database that was just created in the previous section.

To create the sample account table, you need to do this:

CREATE TABLE account

(

id int(6) PRIMARY KEY UNSIGNED AUTO_INCREMENT PRIMARY KEY,

username varchar(16),

password varchar(16),

email varchar(32),

firstname var(16),

lastname var(16),

);

The example above commands the database to create a table named account. Inside the parentheses, the columns that will be created inside the account table are specified. They are separated with a comma. The first column that was created was the id column.

According to the example, the database needs to create the id column (id). It specified that the type of data that it will contain would be integers with six characters (int(6)). Also, it specified some optional attributes. It said that the id column will be the PRIMARY KEY of the table and its values will AUTO_INCREMENT – these will be discussed later. Also, it specified that the integers or data under it will be UNSIGNED, which means that only positive integers will be accepted.

MySQL Data Types

As mentioned before, databases or RDBMS accept multiple types of data. To make databases clean, it is required that you state the data type that you will input in your table's columns. Aside from that, an RDBMS also needs to know the size of the data that you will enter since it will need to allocate the space it needs to store the data you will put in it. Providing precise information about the size of your data will make your database run optimally.

Below are some of the data types that you will and can store in a MySQL database:

- INT(size) – integer data type. Numbers without fractional components or decimal places. A column with an INT data type can accept any number between -2147483648 to 2147483648. In case that you specified that it will be UNSIGNED, the column will accept any number between 0 to 4294967295. You can specify the number of digits with INT. The maximum is 11 digits – it will include the negative sign (-).

- FLOAT(size, decimal) – float data type. Numbers with fractional components or decimal places. It cannot be UNSIGNED. You can specify the number of digits it can handle and the number of decimal places it will store. If you did not specify the size and number of decimals, MySQL will set it to 10 digits and 2 decimal places (the decimal places is included in the count of the digits). Float can have the maximum of 24 digits.

- TIME – time will be stored and formatted as HH:MM:SS.

- DATE – date will be stored and formatted as YYYY-MM-DD. It will not accept any date before year 1,000. And it will not accept date that exceeds 31 days and 12 months.

- DATETIME – combination of DATE and TIME formatted as YYYY-MM-DD HH:MM:SS.

- TIMESTAMP – formatted differently from DATETIME. Its format is YYYYMMDDHHMMSS. It can only store date and time between 19700101000000 and 20371231235959 (not accurate).

- CHAR(size) – stores strings with fixed size. It can have a size of 1 to 255 characters. It uses static memory allocation, which makes it perform faster than VARCHAR. It performs faster because the database will just multiply its way to reach the location of the data you want instead of searching every byte to find the data that you need. To make the data fixed length, it is padded with spaces after the last character.

- VARCHAR(size) – stores strings with variable length size. It can have a size of 1 to 255 characters. It uses dynamic memory allocation, which is slower than static. However, when using VARCHAR, it is mandatory to specify the data's size.

- BLOB –store BLOBs (Binary Large Objects). Data is stored as byte strings instead of character strings (in contrast to TEXT). This makes it possible to store images, documents, or other files in the database.

- TEXT – store text with a length of 65535 characters or less.

- ENUM(x, y, z) – with this, you can specify the values that can be only stored.

INT, BLOB, and TEXT data types can be set smaller or bigger. For example, you can use TINYINT instead of INT to store smaller data. TINYINT can only hold values ranging from -128 to 127 compared to INT that holds values ranging from -2147483648 to 2147483647.

The size of the data type ranges from TINY, SMALL, MEDIUM, NORMAL, and BIG.

- TINYINT, SMALLINT, MEDIUMINT, INT, and BIGINT

- TINYBLOB, SMALLBLOB, MEDIUMBLOB, BLOB, and BIGBLOB

- TINYTEXT, SMALLTEXT, MEDIUMTEXT, TEXT, and BIGTEXT

You already know how to create databases and tables. Now, you need to learn how to insert values inside those tables.

INSERT INTO and VALUES

There are two ways to insert values in your database. Below is the syntax for the first method:

INSERT INTO <name of table>

VALUES (<value 1>, <value 2>, <value 3>);

The same result be done by:

INSERT INTO <name of table>

(<column 1>, <column 2>, <column 3>)

VALUES (<value 1>, <value 2>, <value 3>);

Take note that the first method will assign values according to the arrangement of your columns in the tables. In case you do not want to enter a data to one of the columns in your table, you will be forced to enter an empty value.

On the other hand, if you want full control of the INSERT operation, it will be much better to indicate the name of the corresponding columns that will be given data. Take note that the database will assign the values you will write with respect of the arrangement of the columns in your query.

For example, if you want to insert data in the example account table, you need to do this:

INSERT INTO account

(username, password, email, firstname, lastname)

VALUES

("Johnnyxxx", "123abc", "jjxxx@gmail.com, "Johnny", "Stew");

The statement will INSERT one entry to the database. You might have noticed that the example did not include a value for the ID field. You do not need to do that since the ID field has the AUTO_INCREMENT attribute. The database will be the one to generate a value to it.

SELECT and FROM

To check if the entry you sent was saved to the database, you can use SELECT. As mentioned before, the SELECT statement will retrieve all the data that you want from the database. Its syntax is:

SELECT <column 1> FROM <name of table>;

If you use this in the example account table and you want to get all the usernames in it, you can do it by:

SELECT username FROM account;

In case that you want to multiple records from two or more fields, you can do that by specifying another column. For example:

SELECT username, email FROM account;

WHERE

Unfortunately, using SELECT alone will provide you with tons of data. And you do not want that all the time. To filter out the results you want or to specify the data you want to receive, you can use the WHERE clause. For example:

SELECT <column 1> FROM <name of table>

WHERE <column> <operator> <value>;

If ever you need to get the username of all the people who have Johnny as their first name in the account table, you do that by:

SELECT username FROM account

WHERE firstname = "Johnny";

In the query above, the database will search all the records in the username column that has the value Johnny on the firstname column. The query will return Johnnyxxx and j_sasaki.

LIMIT

What if you only need a specific number of records to be returned? You can use the LIMIT clause for that. For example:

SELECT <column 1> FROM <name of table>

LIMIT <number>;

If you only want one record from the email column to be returned when you use SELECT on the account table, you can do it by:

SELECT email FROM account

LIMIT 1;

You can the LIMIT clause together with the WHERE clause for you to have a more defined search. For example:

SELECT username FROM account

WHERE firstname = "Johnny"

LIMIT 1;

Instead of returning two usernames that have Johnny in the firstname field, it will only return one.

UPDATE and SET

What if you made a mistake and you want to append an entry on your table? Well, you can use UPDATE for that. For example:

UPDATE <name of table>

SET <column 1>=<value 1>, <column 1>=<value 1>, <column 1>=<value 1>

WHERE <column> <operator> <value>;

In the example account table, if you want to change the name of all the people named Master to a different one, you can do that by:

UPDATE account

SET firstname="David"

WHERE firstname="Master";

Take note, you can perform an UPDATE without the WHERE clause. However, doing so will make the database think that you want to UPDATE all the records in the table. Remember that it is a bit complex to ROLLBACK changes in MySQL, so be careful.

DELETE

If you do not to remove an entire row, you can use DELETE. However, if you just want to delete or remove one piece of data in a column, it is better to use UPDATE and place a blank value instead. To perform a DELETE, follow this syntax:

DELETE FROM <name of table>

WHERE <column> <operator> <value>;

If you want to delete the first row in the account table, do this:

DELETE FROM account

WHERE id = 1;

Just like with the UPDATE statement, make sure that you use the WHERE clause when using DELETE. If not, all the rows in your table will disappear.

TRUNCATE TABLE

If you just want to remove all the data inside your table and keep all the settings that you have made to it you need to use TRUNCATE TABLE. This is the syntax for it:

TRUNCATE TABLE <name of table>;

If you want to do that to the account table, do this by entering:

TRUNCATE TABLE account;

DROP TABLE and DROP DATABASE

Finally, if you want to remove a table or database, you can use DROP. Below are examples on how to DROP the account table and sample database.

DROP TABLE account;

DROP DATABASE sample;

Chapter 5: MySQL and PHP

You already know how to manage a MySQL server to the most basic level. Now, it is time to use all those statements and use PHP to communicate with the MySQL server.

To interact or access a MySQL database, you need to send SQL queries to it. There are multiple ways you can do that. But if you want to do it in the web or your website, you will need to use a server side scripting language. And the best one to use is PHP.

In PHP, you can communicate to a MySQL server by using PDO (PHP Data Objects), MySQL extension, or MySQLi extension. Compared to MySQLi extension, PDO is a better choice when communicating with a MySQL database. However, in this book, only MySQLi extension will be discussed since it is less complex and easier to use.

Connecting to a MySQL database:

Before you can do or say anything to a MySQL server or a database, you will need to connect to it first. To do that, follow this example:

```php
<?php
$dbservername = "localhost";
$dbusername = "YourDataBaseUserName";
$dbpassword = "YourPassword12345";

// Create a new connection object
$dbconnection = new mysqli($dbservername, $ dbusername, $ dbpassword);

// Check if connection was successful
if ($dbconnection->connect_error) {
    die("Connection failed/error: " . $dbconnection->connect_error);
}
echo "Connected successfully to database";
?>
```

In this example, you are using PHP's MySQLi to connect to your database. If you are going to test the code in the server that you installed in your computer, use localhost for your database's server name.

By the way, to prevent hackers on any random internet surfers to edit or access your databases, your MySQL server will require you to set a username and password. Every time you connect to it, you will need to include it to the parameters of the mysqli object.

In the example, you have created an object under the mysqli class. All the information that the server will send to you will be accessible in this object.

The third block of code is used to check if your connection request encountered any trouble. As you can see, the if statement is checking whether the connect_error property of the object $dbconnection contains a value. If it does, the code will be terminated and return an error message.

On the other hand, if the connect_error is null, the code will proceed and echo a message that will tell the user that the connection was successful.

Closing a connection

To close a mysqli object's connection, just invoke its close() method. For example:

$dbconnection->close();

Creating a new MySQL Database

```php
<?php
$dbservername = "localhost";
$dbusername = "YourDataBaseUserName";
$dbpassword = "YourPassword12345";

// Create a new connection object
$dbconnection = new mysqli($dbservername, $ dbusername, $ dbpassword);

// Check if connection was successful
```

```php
if ($dbconnection->connect_error) {
    die("Connection failed/error: " . $dbconnection->connect_error);
}


// Creating a Database

$dbSQL = "CREATE DATABASE YourDatabaseName";

if ($dbconnection->query($dbSQL) === TRUE) {

        echo "YourDatabaseName was created.";

}
else {

        echo "An error was encountered while creating your database: "
. $dbconnection->error;

}

$dbconnection->close();
?>
```

Before you request a database to be created, you must connect to your MySQL server first. Once you establish a connection, you will need to tell your server to create a database by sending an SQL query.

The $dbSQL variable was created to hold the query string that you will send. You do not need to do this, but creating a variable for your queries is good practice since it will make your code more readable. If you did not create a variable holder for your SQL, you can still create a database by:

$dbconnection->query("CREATE DATABASE YourDatabaseName")

The if statement was used to both execute the query method of $dbconnection and to check if your server will be able to do it. If it does, it will return a value of TRUE. The if statement will inform you that you were able to create your database.

On the other hand, if it returns false or an error instead, the example code will return a message together with the error.

Once the database was created, the connection was closed.

Interacting with a Database

Once you create a database, you can now send SQL queries and do some operations in it. Before you do that, you need to connect to the server and then specify the name of the database, which you want to interact with, in the parameters of the mysqli class when creating a mysqli object. For example:

```php
<?php
$dbservername = "localhost";
$dbusername = "YourDataBaseUserName";
$dbpassword = "YourPassword12345";

$dbname = "sample"

// Create a new connection object
$dbconnection = new mysqli($dbservername, $ dbusername, $ dbpassword, $sample);

// Check if connection was successful
if ($dbconnection->connect_error) {
    die("Connection failed/error: " . $dbconnection->connect_error);
}
echo "Connected successfully to database";
?>
```

phpMyAdmin

In case you do not want to rely on code to create and manage your databases, you can use the phpMyAdmin tool. Instead of relying on sending SQL queries, you will be given a user interface that is easier to use and reduces the chances of error since you do not need to type SQL and create typos. Think of it as Microsoft Access with a different interface.

The tool will also allow you to enter SQL if you want to and it will provide you with the SQL queries that it has used to perform the requests you make. Due to that, this tool will help you get more familiar with SQL. And the best thing about it is that it is free.

On the other hand, you can use phpMyAdmin to check the changes you made to the database while you are studying MySQL. If you do that, you will be able to debug faster since you do not need to redisplay or create a code for checking the contents of your database using PHP.

Conclusion

Thank you again for purchasing this book!

I hope this book was able to help you to master the fundamentals of MySQL programming.

The next step is to learn more about:

- Advanced SQL Statements and Clauses

- Attributes

- The MySQLi Class

- PHP Data Object

- Security Measures in MySQL

- Importing and Exporting MySQL Databases

- Different Applications of MySQL

Those topics will advance your MySQL programming skills. Well, even with the things you have learned here, you will already be capable of doing great things. With the knowledge you have, you can already create an online chat application, social network site, and online games!

That is no exaggeration. If you do not believe that, well, check out the sample codes that experts share on the web. You will be surprised how simple their codes are.

Finally, if you enjoyed this book, please take the time to share your thoughts and post a review on Amazon. We do our best to reach out to readers and provide the best value we can. Your positive review will help us achieve that. It'd be greatly appreciated!

Thank you and good luck!

Check Out My Other Books

Below you'll find some of my other popular books that are popular on Amazon and Kindle as well. Simply click on the links below to check them out. Alternatively, you can visit my author page on Amazon to see other work done by me.

Android Programming in a Day

Python Programming in a Day

C Programming Success in a Day

C Programming Professional Made Easy

JavaScript Programming Made Easy

PHP Programming Professional Made Easy

C ++ Programming Success in a Day

Windows 8 Tips for Beginners

HTML Professional Programming Made Easy

Programming Box Set #78: Android Programming in a Day & MySQL Programming Professional Made Easy

If the links do not work, for whatever reason, you can simply search for these titles on the Amazon website to find them.